Panchatantra on Stage

Plays for Children

Julie Meighan

First published in 2016 by

JemBooks

Cork,

Ireland

www.drama-in-ecce.com

ISBN: 978-0-9568966-5-0

All rights reserved.

No part of this book may be reproduced or utilised in any form or by any electronic, digital or mechanical means, including information storage, photocopying, filming, recording, video recording and retrieval systems, without prior permission in writing from the publisher. The only exception is by a reviewer, who may quote short excerpts in a review. The moral rights of the author have been asserted.

Text Copyright © 2016, Julie Meighan

Panchatantra on Stage

Plays for Children

Julie Meighan

JemBooks

Julie Meighan

About the Author

Julie Meighan is a lecturer in Drama in Education at the Cork Institute of Technology. She has taught Drama to all age groups and levels. She is the author of the Amazon bestselling *Drama Start: Drama Activities, Plays and Monologues for Young Children (Ages 3 -8)* ISBN 978-0956896605, *Drama Start Two: Drama Activities and Plays for Children (Ages 9-12)* ISBN 978-0-9568966-1-2 and *Stage Start: 20 Plays for Children (Ages 3-12)* ISBN 978-0956896629.

Panchatantra on Stage

Table of Contents

About The Author	IV
Table Of Contents	V
Introduction	VI
About The Panchatantra	VII
The Four Friends And The Hunter	1
The Blue Jackal	3
The Monkey And The Crocodile	6
The Frog And The Two Fish	9
The Bullock And The Lion	11
The Old Man, Tiger And Jackal	14
The Rabbit And The Lion	17
The Sage And The Mouse	19
The Elephants And The Mice	21
The Tortoise And The Eagle	24
The Crane And The Crafty Crab	26
The Donkey And The Jackal	28
The Jackal And The Elephant	31
The Thief, The Brahmin And The Demon	33
The Owl And Crow	35
The Bug And The Flea	37
The Turtle And The Two Swans	39
The Monkey And The Sparrows	41

Introduction

This book consists of eighteen plays that are based on the old Indian book the Panchatantra. Each play is between five and ten minutes long. The plays can be used for performance, readers' theatre or to promote reading in groups. The plays are simple so it is very easy for young children to memorise their lines. The cast list is flexible – more characters can be added and existing characters can be changed or omitted depending on the size and requirements of the group. Most of the characters can be on stage throughout the play, with children walking to the centre of the stage when it is time to say their lines. The teacher/leader can assume the role of the storyteller/s if the children can't read or are not at the reading level required.

Props/costumes/stage directions:
There is a minimal amount of props required to stage these plays. The costumes for all the plays are or can be very simple. For example, the children can just wear a colour that represents their animal, wear a mask or use some face paint. A word of advice: if the children wear masks, make sure they don't cover their mouths as it would make it difficult to hear them speak. All suggestions for stage directions are included in brackets and italics.

I hope you enjoy performing or reading the following plays as much as my drama groups have over the years.
BREAK A LEG!

About the Panchatantra

The Panchatantra is one of the world's oldest books and even today remains one of the most popular works of literature. It originated in India and was initially written in the Indian languages of Sanskrit and Pali. It is a collection of stories with morals that aim to help people to succeed in life. It is believed to written around 300 B.C by Vishnu Sharma. The Panchatantra has been translated into fifty languages and there are over two hundred different versions available.

Background to the Panchatantra:
The legend behind the Panchatantra is there once lived a king who had three sons. The sons were not very bright. The king was worried how they would rule his kingdom justly and fairly when he died. The King asked a Brahmin called Vishnu Sharma to help his sons become more knowledgeable. Sharma decided pass on his wisdom by the use of stories. In these stories, all animals take on human qualities. Pancha means five and tantra means ways or principles.
The five books or principles are:
Book 1: The separation of friends. *(The Bull and the Lion.)*
Book 2: The gaining of friends. *(The Four Friends and the Hunter)*
Book 3: Conflict and solutions. *(The Owl and Crow)*
Book 4: Loss of gains. *(The Monkey and the Crocodile.)*
Book 5: Ill considered actions. *(The Sage and the Mouse.)*

Write your own Panchatantra tale:

Book/principle:

Title:

Characters:

Hero/es:

Villain/s:

Other character/s:

Setting:

Problem:

Solution:

Trickery:

Moral:

To help you write your own tale, the following is a list of the most common characters found in the Panchatantra:
Brahmin
King
Hunter
Sage
Lion
Tiger
Jackal
Crow
Fish
Deer
Owl
Hare
Monkey

Panchatantra on Stage

Crocodile
Rat
Dove
Pigeon
Tortoise
Mongoose
Mouse

The Four Friends and the Hunter

Characters: Three storytellers, mouse, crow, deer, turtle, two hunters.

Storyteller 1: Long, long, ago there lived three friends in the jungle.
Storyteller 2: There was a deer, a crow, and a mouse.
(Deer, crow and mouse are all jumping and playing with each other.)
Storyteller 2: They always played together and looked out for one another. One day a turtle came along.
(Turtle plods slowly towards the three friends.)
Turtle: Hello everyone, may I play with you and be your friend.
Deer: of course.
Crow: You are most welcome.
Mouse: Come and play with us now.
Storyteller 1: Then, suddenly the mouse stopped and sniffed and he said…
Mouse: I smell some hunters.
Deer: What will we do?
Crow: Quick let's get out of here.
(Enter two hunters looking for prey.)
Storyteller 2: The deer darted through the jungle.
Storyteller 3: The crow flew high up into the sky.
Storyteller 2: And the mouse scarpered into a hole but the turtle moved very slowly indeed.
Hunter 1: Oh no! We just missed that juicy deer.
Hunter 2: Never mind *(points to turtle)* we can catch that turtle and we will have delicious turtle stew for dinner.
(The hunters capture the turtle. They put a net over him and start to pull.)
Storyteller 3: The turtle's three friends were very worried.
Mouse: They have caught the turtle?
Crow: How will we save him?
Deer: Listen, I have an idea. *(They huddle up together and whisper to each other.)*
Storyteller 1: The crow flew up into the sky and spotted the two hunters carrying the turtle near the river.

Crow: *(shouts down and points)* There, they are.
Storyteller 2: The deer darted through the jungle and when she came to path she lay down as if she were dead.
Hunter 1: Do you see what I see?
Hunter 2: Yes, it is a dead deer.
Hunter: Now, we really will eat like kings, tonight.
Hunter 2: And we can sell its beautiful skin to the nearest bidder.
Storyteller 3: In their excitement they put down the turtle.
Storyteller 1: This was exactly what the deer had planned.
(Mouse sneaks out very quietly and starts to gnaw at the rope)
Turtle: I'm free. Thank you mouse. You are a true friend.
Mouse: Come with me.
(Turtle moves slowly and then disappears into the river and the mouse runs into the jungle.)
Storyteller 1: Just as the hunters were going to lean down and take the deer, she got up and darted off into the jungle.
Hunter 1: She wasn't dead at all.
Hunter 2: Never mind, we still have the turtle.
Storyteller 2: They turned around and saw that the trap was empty and the turtle was gone.
Hunter1: The trap is empty.
Hunter 2: *(sighs)* Looks like we will go hungry again tonight.
Storytellers: The moral of this story is a friend in need is a friend in deed.

The Blue Jackal

Characters: Three storytellers, greedy jackal, lion, two guard dogs, elephant, monkey, tiger, snake and two or more jackals.

Storyteller 1: A long time ago there was a large jungle near a very long river.
Storyteller 2: The forest was ruled by a brave lion.
Storyteller 2: On the other side of the river was a village.
Lion: No animals must enter the village. It is the law of the jungle.
Storyteller 1: Not everyone listened to the lion.
Storyteller 2: There was a very greedy jackal that broke the law every day looking for food.
Greedy Jackal: I love the food that the villagers cook. I must be careful if the villagers and their dogs catch me they will be very anger.
Storyteller 3: One day the jackal went to the village. He saw a lovely cake cooling by the window of a villager's hut.
(He was just about to stick his large teeth into the cake when he heard some barking. It was the villagers' guard dogs.)
Guard dog 1: Woof woof, I smell something.
Guard dog 2: It is that lovely cake by the window.
Guard dog 1: No, it is not the cake. It smells like … like a …
(Guard dog 2 spots the Jackal.)
Guard dog 2: Like a jackal.
Guard dog 1: Yes that's it. How did you know?
Guard dog 2: Because he is about to eat the cake. *(He points to the jackal.)*
Guard dog 1: Quick after him.
Storyteller 1: The jackal who was about to take a large bite of cake, dropped it and ran.
Storyteller 2: In his hurry to get away he fell into a tub of blue dye. He stayed hidden.
Guard dog 1: He must have got away.

Guard dog 2: Let's go back to the village and have some cake.
Story teller 1: The jackal finally stuck his head out the tub when he knew it was safe.
Storyteller 2: He was dyed blue from head to foot.
Jackal: *(looking at himself)* I look so different. Now, I can fool all my friends in the jungle.
Storyteller 1: When jackal returned all the other animals were amazed.
Elephant: Who are you?
Monkey: Where did you come from?
Snake: We have never seen an animal like you in the jungle.
Storyteller 2: The jackal remained quite and marched up, to the brave lion who was the king of the jungle.
Lion: *(frowning)* Why have you come here? What do you want?
Jackal: *(to himself)* This is great; the other animals don't recognise me.
Jackal: I am a very special animal with special powers. I have been sent by Lord Indra. You must do as I say.
Tiger *(suspiciously)* What if we don't do as you say?
Jackal: Then, the forest will be destroyed with all the animals in it. Only I can save you from this terrible fate.
Tiger: Well then we will make you our king and do whatever you say.
(All the animals bow.)
Jackal: I want food and plenty of it and you must banish jackals from this jungle.
Storyteller 1: The greedy jackal knew if the other jackals saw him they would recognise him.
(The animals bring him food and the lion goes and tells the jackals to leave the jungle.)
Storyteller 2: Lion summoned all the jackals in the jungle.
Lion: Jackals, you must leave the jungle at once.
Jackal 1: Let's go to the top of the mountain.
(They travel to top of the mountain.)
Jackal 2: Why did Lord Indra's animal banish us from the forest?
Storyteller 1: Some of the jackals started howling and when the greedy jackal heard them he stood up and started howling out of habit.
Monkey: He is howling like a common jackal.

Lion: That's because he is just a common jackal.
Elephant: You fooled us.
Lion: How dare you. You must leave the jungle, never to return again
Greedy Jackal: I'm sorry.
All animals: It is too late. Go!
Storytellers: The moral is you can change your appearance but not your true nature.

Julie Meighan

The Monkey and the Crocodile

Characters: Three storytellers, the crocodile, the crocodile's wife and the monkey.

Storyteller 1: Once upon a time there lived a crocodile that lived in the river Ganges in India.
(Crocodile enters stage swimming slowly.)
Storyteller 2: On both sides of the Ganges there were large music fruit trees.
Storyteller 3: A monkey lived in one of the trees. He ate fruit all day.
(Monkey mimes eating fruit.)
Monkey: These fruits are so delicious and juicy I'm so lucky to live in a fruit tree.
(Crocodile sits under the tree for shade.)
Crocodile: It is very hot I think I will sit under this tree and sleep in the shade. *(Looks up.)* The fruits on tree look so delicious. I wish I could climb the tree and pick some.
Monkey: *(climbs down from the tree)* Since you are resting under my tree, you are my guest. Please come and taste some of my delicious fruits.
Narrator: The monkey plucked the juiciest fruit off the tree and gave it to the crocodile.
Crocodile: Oh thank you Monkey you are so kind.
Monkey: You are welcome. Come again, any time.
Storyteller: Soon, the crocodile came every day. They would eat the fruit and talk to one another for hours.
(Crocodile and the monkey mime having a conversation and eating lots of fruits.)
Storyteller: One day as the crocodile was leaving to swim home. The monkey gave him some fruit.
Monkey: Crocodile give these fruits to your wife. I plucked them especially for her.

Storyteller: The crocodile swam home and gave the fruit to his wife, She was very happy.
(Crocodile swims home and gives his wife the fruit.)
Crocodile's wife: These fruits are delicious. I have never tasted such sweet fruit in all my life. Where did you get them from?
Crocodile: I got them from my friend the monkey. He lives in the fruit tree so he knows which ones are the sweetest.
Crocodile's wife: Does the monkey eat fruit every day?
Crocodile: Yes, only the sweetest and juiciest ones. Why do you ask?
Crocodile's wife: Because that means his heart must be so sweet. If I eat his heart I would remain young and beautiful forever. You must steal the monkey's heart and give it to me.
Crocodile: But he is my good friend. He is my only friend. It would be unfair for me to steal his heart.
Crocodile's wife: *(gets angry)* If you loved me you would do it.
Crocodile: Do not get anger my dear, I will do as you wish.
Storyteller: The next day the crocodile swam to the riverbank and reached the tree where the monkey lived.
Monkey: Crocodile, you are late today. I thought you weren't coming.
Crocodile: My wife has made a meal for you. She has invited you to tea because she wants to thank you for giving her your beautiful sweet fruit.
Monkey: That's very kind of her but I'm a land animal, I can't swim.
Crocodile: We live on a sand bank just jump on my back and I'll take you there.
Storyteller: The monkey hopped on the crocodile's back and away they went.
Monkey: Slow down, Croc. You are going too fast.
Crocodile: I'm sorry Monkey but I have to go fast because my wife wants to eat your heart for her tea.
Monkey: Oh Croc, you should have told me this before we left. I always keep my heart in the hollow of the tree for safe keeping.
Crocodile: I'll take you back to the tree and you can collect your heart.
Monkey: That would be great.

Storyteller: Crocodile turns and swims back to the tree where the monkey lives upon reaching the bank the monkey jumps off the crocodiles back and clambers up the tree. After a while the crocodile says…..

Crocodile: Monkey, you must have found your heart by now. My wife will get angry if we don't arrive soon.

Monkey: You are so foolish crocodile. Don't you know your heart is within yourself? It was a trick to save my life. Now leave my tree and never come back again.

Storyteller: The crocodile left empty handed.

(Crocodile's wife looks very angry.)

Storytellers: The moral of the story is at times presence of mind pays well.

The Frog and the Two Fish

Characters: Three storytellers, frog, fish 1, fish 2, fisherman 1, fisherman 2, crab 1, crab 2, crab 3, crab 4, crab 5, frog's wife and the wise old fish.

Storyteller 1: Once upon a time there lived two fish in a lake.
(The fish are playing with one another swimming and jumping around.)
Storyteller 2: They were very good friends with one of the frogs that lived nearby.
(Frog enters and joins the fish. They are having fun.)
Storyteller 3: Every day, they would play with each other by the far end of the lake. One day while they were playing some fisherman walked by.
Frog: Look, fish.
Fish 1: Who are they?
Frog: They are fishermen. They have finally found our lake and they will catch us all
Fish 2: Why will they try to catch us? What use are we to them.
Frog: They will catch us and feed us to their people.
Fisherman 1: I have never seen this lake before.
Fisherman 2: We are lucky we found it. It is full of fish.
Fisherman 1: We must come back in the morning and catch some fish.
Fisherman 2: What a good idea.
Fish: We are frightened. What will we do?
Frog: We must call a meeting with all the lake creatures.
Frog: Everyone gather round.
Crab: What is all this fuss?
Frog 2: I was enjoying the sun and relaxing.
Crab 2: what do you want frog.
Frog: We have just seen two fishermen. They are coming back to the lake in the morning with fishing nets. We have to get out here and find a safer place to live.
Crab 3: But this is the only safe place we know.
Crab 4: We have nowhere else to go.

Crab 5: Why don't we ask the wise old fish?
Crab 1: He always knows what to do.
Frog: Old wise fish what shall we do? If the fishermen come back tomorrow we will all surely die.
Wise Old Fish: Don't worry Frog. The world is safe because dreams of snakes and evil men do not come true. Nothing will happen to us.
Crab 2: Well, we should stay here in the lake.
Crab 3: The wise old fish has spoken.
Frog: I think we are not safe and we should move to a safer place.
Fish 1: The wise old fish is very wise.
Fish 2: Everything he says is true.
Frog: Well, I'm not staying here. Please, come with me.
Fish 1: We will stay here.
Fish 2: The lake is our home. You go if you wish.
Storyteller: The frog was very upset that his best friends had abandoned him.
Storyteller: However he packed his bags. He and his wife left the lake.
Storyteller 3: The next morning the two fishermen came back to the lake. They caught the crabs, the two fishes and the wise old fish in their net.
Fisherman 1: Looks like we will have a delicious sea food pie for dinner tonight.
Fisherman 2: What a good idea it was to come back here.
Fish 1: We should have listened to the frog.
Fish 2: We should have trusted him more than the wise old fish.
(The fishermen drag their catch off stage.)
Frog: Look at my poor friends. No one can save them now. Why didn't they listen to me?
Frog's wife: We all make decisions and we have to pay the price of those decisions. We would be in the same situation if we did not leave.
Storytellers: At the first hint of danger save yourself.

The Bullock and the Lion

Characters: Three narrators, Merchant, servant 1, servant 2, bullock, deer, rabbit, lion, jackal 1, jackal 2.

Narrator: Once upon a time there was a merchant who lived in the south of India.
Narrator: The merchant was wealthy and prosperous but he was not happy
Narrator: He wanted more. One day while he was counting his money. He said
Merchant: Oh, how I wish I had more money. The wealthy you are the more money you seem to have. Even your enemies become your friends when you are rich.
Narrator: He spent all his time thinking of different ways to make more money?
Merchant: I have it, servants come here now!
(Servants come running in.)
Merchant: We are going to go to another town to sell our wares.
Servant 1: Why can't we sell our wares here in this town?
Merchant: Everyone in this town knows me and there are always trying to bargain. If we go to a town faraway we can sell our wares at a much higher price and I will become richer.
Servant 2: Master, we will never be able to carry all these wares. What shall we do?
Merchant: Get the bullock from the shed. He is big and strong and he will carry everything.
Servant 1: Bullock, come here. *(Bullock comes on stage. The savants start loading the wares on him.)*
Bullock: This is too much. I can't carry all these wares.
Servant 2: The master has ordered us to bring as much as we can. He wants to become rich,
Narrator: So off they went to seek to their fortune in a faraway town.
Narrator: The sun was shining brightly and as midday approached it got hotter and hotter.

Narrator: The bullock was tired and ill and eventually he collapses due to the heat.
Servant 1: The bullock has collapsed. What shall we do now?
Merchant: I will go ahead and set up everything in the far away town. You stay here with the bullock and when he is better follow me.
Bullock: I have worked hard and suffered greatly all my life. Please, leave me here to die in peace
Servant 1: He will be dead soon and night is coming.
Servant 2: Let's leave him behind and continue on our journey.
Narrator: The servants left the bullock to die alone and off they went to the faraway town.
Narrator: Fortunately the bullock didn't die. He slept soundly. When he woke he drank from the nearby river. He ate some of the juicy grass.
Narrator 3: He got stronger and stronger and he explored the forest. What the bullock didn't know was this forest was ruled by a fierce lion.
Lion: I am the king of the forest. All the animals must bow before and do as I wish.
Rabbit: Yes, master
Elephant: Yes master
Deer: Yes master.
Lion: Get me food.
(They hear a might roars.)
Lion: What was that?
Rabbit: It sounds like a mighty beast.
Deer: A fierce beast
Elephant: A scary beast.
Narrator: What the animals didn't know it was the sound of the bullock mooing.
Bullock: Moo, moo, at last I'm free. I'm celebrating moo, moo,
Narrator: Just then two jackals passed by.
Jackal 1: Whatever is the matter?
Lion: There is a mighty, fierce, scary beast roaming the jungle. We are so frightened.
Jackal 1: What could have made our mighty King turned into a timid mouse?
Jackal 2: Let's find out.

Narrator: They go behind the tree and the see the bullock
Jackal 1: What is that creature?
Bullock: Moo, moo.
Jackal 2: I never heard such a noise.
Narrator: There were filled with fear and they raced back to the other animals.
Lion: There is nothing for it but we have to make this new creature King of the Jungle
Narrator: The animals approached him and gave him the crown.
Bullock: Thank you so much everyone. My life has changed so much.
Narrators: The moral of the story that situations changes and never remain the same.

Julie Meighan

The Old Man, Tiger and Jackal

Characters: Tiger, Old Man, Jackal, Tree, Camel, Crocodile, Eagle, three Storytellers and three Villagers.

Storyteller 1: Once upon a time in a little village in India.....
Storyteller 2: .....There lived a tiger that scared all the villagers.
(All the villagers mime doing some type of work. They can be digging holes, feeding cattle/chickens, cooking, chopping down trees, putting up fences, etc... The tiger walks around roaring and scaring the villagers.)
(Tiger moves to stage left.)
Tiger: *(yawns)* Scaring all those frightened villagers is a very tiring job. I think I will go for a snooze.
(Tiger stretches and falls asleep.)
Villager 1: We must do something about the scary tiger.
Villager 2: We could capture him with this net. *(Points to a net.)*
Villager 3: And then we put him in this wooden cage. *(Points to a wooden cage.)*
Storyteller 1: So all the villagers worked together to capture the tiger with the net and locked him in the wooden cage.
Storyteller 2: The tiger snarled and snarled but he could not get out of the wooden cage.
Villager 1: Now you won't be able to scare us anymore.
Villagers: Ha, ha, ha. *(Villagers leave the tiger and go back to doing their jobs.)*
Tiger: Oh dear. How will I get out of here? *(He starts to moan.)* *(Old man passes by.)*
Tiger: Old man, help me. The nasty villagers locked me up. Now I am hungry and thirsty. Please, let me out so I can drink some water from the cold stream.
Old Man: I would love to help you but I am not a fool. I know if I let you out you will eat me.
Tiger: Oh no, I wouldn't. I would be so grateful to you.
Old Man: I will let you out but you must promise not to eat me.
Tiger: I promise.

Storyteller 2: So the old man opened the wooden cage.
(Tiger pounces on the man, he grabs him and he roars loudly.)
Tiger: I am going to eat you up.
Old Man: You promised you wouldn't eat me. Would you really eat the man that saved your life?
Tiger: Of course, I would.
Old Man: *(thinking quickly)* why don't we ask five different beings whether they think it is fair that you eat me?
(Tiger thinks for a moment and then nods his head and says that's fair.)
Storyteller 3: They walked in the midday sun and it got hotter and hotter, (they rub their brows) so they decided to rest under the tree. The old man looked up at the tree and said:
Old Man: Tree, I helped the tiger escape from a wooden cage and now he wants to eat me. Do you think this is fair?
Tree: People show me no gratitude. They sit under my branches all day to shade themselves from the sun but as soon as night falls they chop down my branches for fire wood. So yes I think it is fair that the tiger eats you.
(They get up and leave and the tiger looks smug. A camel passes them.)
Old Man: Camel, I helped the tiger escape from a wooden cage and now he wants to eat me. Do you think this is fair?
Camel: I work really hard but my master doesn't care. Nobody shows me any gratitude. So yes, I think it is fair that the tiger eats you.
(An Eagle passes by.)
Old Man: Eagle, I helped the tiger escape from a wooden cage and now he wants to eat me. Do you think this is fair?
Eagle: People steal my eggs and no one shows me any gratitude so yes, I think it is fair that the tiger eats you.
(On the riverbank they pass a crocodile.)
Old Man: Crocodile, I helped the tiger escape from a wooden cage and now he wants to eat me. Do you think this is fair?
Crocodile: Everyday, people want to kill me to make shoes and handbags. Nobody shows me any gratitude so yes; I think it is fair that the tiger eats you.
(The tiger is now looking very smug and the man looks very downhearted.)
Tiger: Well it looks like everyone thinks it is fair that I eat you. (He grabs the old man and opens his mouth.)
Old Man: Hold on, we need to ask one more being.

(A Jackal passes by.)
Old Man: Jackal, I helped the tiger escape from a cage and now he wants to eat me. Do you think this is fair?
Jackal: Well, that is difficult to answer. What type of cage was it?
Tiger: A wooden one.
Jackal: I can't really answer unless I see the cage.
Storyteller 1: The tiger and the old man take him to the cage.
Jackal: Now, where exactly were you standing?
Old Man: Here.
Jackal: And you, Tiger? Where were you standing?
Tiger: Inside the cage.
Jackal: Could you show me so I can get a better picture?
(Tiger enters the cage and the jackal closes the door.)
Jackal: One more question: was the door locked?
Old Man: Yes, Just like this. He bolts the door.
Jackal: Now, Old Man, go home and Tiger, you can stay inside the cage. The old man helped you and you were so ungrateful you tried to eat him. I hope you stay there for a very long time.
(Old Man and the Jackal walk away leaving the Tiger locked in the cage.)
Tiger: Oh no, I have been tricked. (He starts to cry.)

The Rabbit and the Lion

Characters: Three narrators, the rabbit, the lion, deer, elephant.

Narrator1: Once upon a time in a jungle in India.
Narrator 2: There lived a lion. He was very powerful and very cruel.
Narrator 3: He hunted and killed a lot of animals in the jungle. Sometimes he just hunted and killed for fun.
Rabbit: We have to stop this unnecessary killing.
Elephant: How can we stop the lion? He is too powerful.
Deer: Why don't we have a meeting with the lion?
Fox: And see if we can reach an agreement.
Narrator 1: So all the animals in the jungle gathered together and invited the lion to the meeting.
Lion: What do you want?
Rabbit: Your majesty we are happy for you to be the King of the Jungle.
Deer: We are happy for you to rule the jungle,
Elephant: We understand that you need to kill us for food.
Lion: Why, that is most kind and understanding of you.
Rabbit: But you are killing animals for fun and not when you are hungry. And if you don't stop there won't be any animals left in jungle.
Lion: Well, what do you suggest?
Rabbit: We decided that we will send you an animal a day to your den. You can kill and eat it. You won't have to go to the bother of hunting.
Lion: Well, that sounds like a good idea.
Narrator 3: The day arrived where it was the rabbits turn to go to the lion's den.
Rabbit: I don't want to go.
Other animals: You have to go if you don't go he will kill the other animals. It was your idea.
Rabbit: I better go then.

Lion: Why are you late?
Rabbit: *(out of breath)* Your majesty it was not my fault. Another lion chased me no wanted to eat me. He said he was king of the jungle.
Lion: I'm the only King of the Jungle. Who is he? Take me to him at once. I shall kill him.
Rabbit: Come with me. I will show you where he lives.
Narrator1: The lion followed the rabbit through the jungle.
Narrator 2: They reached a well.
Rabbit: He lives here.
Narrator 3. The rabbit roared and looked into the well. He saw his own reflection looking back at him.
Lion: I see him.
Rabbit: There can only be one King of the jungle. You must kill him.
Narrator 1: The lion jumped into the well and was taken away.
(The rabbit went off and told his friends what had happened.)
(They all had a big party to celebrate.)

The Sage and the Mouse

Characters: Three storytellers, mouse, sage, cat, fox, tiger.

Storyteller 1: Once upon there was a sage.
Storyteller 2: Every day, he would give spiritual teachings in the forest.
Storyteller 3: All the animals come to listen to him.
Sage: OMMMMMMMMMMMMMMMMMMM!
(Animals nodding there heads.)
Storyteller 1: Everyday there was a little mouse that came to listen to what the sage had to say.
Mouse: The sage is so wise.
Storyteller 2: One day the Mouse was walking through the forest after the sage's meeting. There was a cat waiting behind a tree.
Cat: Look at that mouse he looks fat and juicy.
(Cat jumps out in front of the mouse.)
Cat: Mouse, I'm very hungry and you look very filling.
Mouse: You can't eat me.
Cat: Try to stop me.
Storyteller 3: The mouse ran as fast as he could to the sage's tree.
Sage: Whatever is the matter, Mouse?
Mouse: Oh, wise old sage. Please help me. The cat wants to eat me.
Storyteller 1: Soon the cat arrived at the sage's tree.
Sage: I will use my spiritual powers to turn you into a bigger cat.
(He turns the mouse into a bigger cat.)
Mouse: Cat, I'm bigger than you now.
(He chases the cat.)
Storyteller 2: The mouse liked being in his new body. He walked around the jungle without being scared of the animals. One day, he met a fox.
Fox: Cat, you look nice and juicy and I'm hungry. I will eat you.
Mouse: You can't eat me.
Fox: Oh yes, I can.

Storyteller 2: The mouse ran to the sage's tree and the fox followed closely behind.
Sage: Whatever is the matter?
Mouse: Oh, wise old sage. Please, help me. The fox wants to eat me.
Sage: I will use my spiritual powers to turn you into a bigger fox.
Mouse: Fox, I'm bigger than you now. He chases the fox.
Storyteller 2: The mouse liked being in his new body. He walked around the jungle without being scared of the other animals. One day, he met a tiger.
Tiger: Fox, you look nice and juicy and I'm hungry. I will eat you.
Mouse: You can't eat me.
Tiger: Oh yes, I can.
Storyteller 2: The mouse ran to the sage's tree and the tiger followed closely behind.
Sage: Whatever is the matter?
Mouse: Oh, wise old sage. Please, help me. The tiger wants to eat me.
Sage: I will use my spiritual powers to turn you into a bigger tiger.
Mouse: Tiger, I'm bigger than you now. He chases the tiger.
Storyteller 2: The mouse liked being in his new body. He walked around the forest as if he was the king.
Storyteller 3: However, he was bothered by sage's powers. He knew that the sage could change back into a little mouse with a click of his fingers.
Mouse: If I eat the sage then I will enjoy his divine powers,
Storyteller 1: He went to the sage's tree.
Sage: Hello mouse, what can I do for you today?
Mouse: Well, I'm very hungry. I'm going to eat you so I can enjoy your great powers.
Storyteller 2: The mouse was just about to pounce on the sage but the sage turned him back into a mouse.
Sage: How dare you mouse! I've turned you back to what you really are - a small, scared mouse.
Mouse: I'm so sorry; please change me back to a tiger.
Sage: No, leave my tree and never come back.

The Elephants and the Mice

Characters: Three storytellers, King Mouse, King Elephant, King, six elephants, six mice, four soldiers.

Storyteller 1: Once upon a time in India there was an earthquake.
Storyteller 2: It left a village in ruins.
Storyteller 3: There was damaged houses and rubble everywhere.
Storyteller 1: All the villagers had left and the village was deserted except for a group of mice.
(The mice come scurrying on the stage.)
Mouse 1: How lucky we are that we found these ruins to live in.
Mouse 2: We are safe here. Nobody will ever bother us.
Mouse 3: *(suddenly, there was a thumping noise.)* What's that noise?
Mouse 4: Oh no, it is a herd of elephants. Everyone quick hide.
(All the mice hide around the stage.)
(Elephants come stomping on to the stage.)
Storyteller 2: There was a lake next to the village.
Storyteller 3: The elephants had no choice but to walk through the village.
Elephant 1: I'm thirsty.
Elephant 2: We are nearly at the lake.
Elephants 3: All we need to do is pass these ruins.
Elephants 4: What's that under my feet?
Elephant 5: It is only some mice.
Elephant 6: Just step over them.
(The mice try to avoid the elephants by running around the stage.)
Mouse 5: Wow! That was close *(he wipes his brow.)*
Mouse 6: We can't keep avoiding the elephants. They are going pass here every day to get to the lake.
Mouse 1: I agree, I think we should have a meeting with the king of the mice.
(The king of the mice enters and all the mice bow.)
King Mouse: You wish to speak to me.
Mouse 2: Yes your majesty. We have a problem.
King Mouse: How can I help?

Mouse 3: The elephants come through the village and they don't look where they are going.
Mouse 4: If they don't stop they will trample us all.
Mouse 5: King Mouse you have to do something
Mouse 6: Or else we will all die
King Mouse: I shall ask the King of the Elephants to help us.
(King Elephants walks on stage.)
King Elephant: I hear you want my help.
King Mouse: *(bows)* Yes, your majesty. We live in the ruins of the village which is near the big lake where the elephants drink their water but every time the herd of elephants pass the village they trample the mice with their massive feet.
King Elephant: What would you like me to do? The elephants have to go to the lake to drink the water and bathe.
King Mouse: All you need to do is suggest they change their route.
King Elephant: Why should they?
King Mouse: Because one day the mice could help you.
King Elephant: *(Laughing)* You mice are too small to help giants like us. I will change the route because you made me laugh so much.
King Mouse: Thank you so much, King Elephant.
Storyteller 1: The elephants changed their route and no longer went through the ruined village.
Storyteller 2: There was a king in a nearby kingdom who decided he needed more elephants for his army.
King: Soldiers, you need to capture more elephants.
Soldiers: Yes, your majesty.
(They go off into the jungle and capture the elephants with nets.)
Soldier 1: I think we have captured enough elephants now.
Soldier 2: The king will be very pleased with us.
Soldier 3: I'm hungry. Let's get something to eat and we can come back later and get the elephants.
Soldier 4: They will never escape from this net.
(Soldiers leave the elephants and move to the other side of the stage and mime eating.)
Elephant 1: What are we going to do?
Elephant 2: We will never get out of here.
King Elephant: I have an idea.

(He trumpets really loudly and the mice come in.)
King Mouse: King Elephant, you called.
King Elephant: The king's soldiers captured us. We are stuck in this net and we can't get out.
King Mouse: Come on, mice. Let's bite through the ropes and free the elephants.
Storyteller 1: Eventually, the elephants broke free.
Storyteller 2: They were very happy and they thanked the mice for their help.
Storyteller 3: The lesson of this story is never estimate people.

Julie Meighan

The Tortoise and the Eagle

Characters: Two storytellers, tortoise, eagle, snail, squirrel, rabbit, crow, dove, robin.

Storyteller 1: There once was a tortoise that lived in a wood.
Storyteller 2: He was never happy.
Tortoise: I'm so bored. All I do all day is plod along. If only I could fly like the birds up in the sky.
(Birds come on stage and fly around. The tortoise looks at them with envy.)
Snail: Tortoise, why are you never happy. You have lots of things to be grateful for.
Tortoise: Like what?
Snail: You have a big hard shell.
Squirrel: You have lots of friends in the woods.
Rabbit: None of us can fly and we are not bored.
Storyteller 1: The tortoise sighed and said…
Tortoise: I don't like being stuck on the ground. I think, I will ask the birds to help me. Birds, birds, could one of you take me up into the sky so I can see the wonders of the world.
(The crow flies down to meet the tortoise.)
Tortoise: Crow, crow, please help me fly.
Crow: No, I will not help you fly. You are too heavy. *(Crow flies off.)*
(Dove flies down to meet the tortoise.)
Tortoise: Dove, dove, please help me fly.
Dove: No I will not help you fly. You have no feathers, you aren't meant to fly. *(Dove flies away.)*
(Robin flies down to meet the tortoise.)
Tortoise: Robin, robin, please help me fly.
Robin: No, I will not help you fly. It is too dangerous. *(Robin flies away.)*
(Eagle flies down to meet the tortoise.)
Tortoise: Eagle, eagle, please help me fly.
Eagle: I will help you fly.
(The eagle picks up the tortoise with his talons and starts to fly.)

Storyteller 2: The tortoise was so frightened he closed his eyes really tightly.

Eagle: Tortoise, you must open your eyes if you want to see the wonders of the world.

Tortoise: I can't open my eyes. I'm too scared. Eagle, please put me down.

(The eagle puts the tortoise down and flies off. The tortoise starts crying.)

Storytellers: The moral of the story is be careful what you wish for.

Julie Meighan

The Crane and the Crafty Crab

Characters: Three narrators, the crane, the crab, five fish.

Narrator 1: Once upon a time there was an old crane. He lived near a large lake in the middle of the jungle.
(Crane is sitting by the lake, looking old and tired. He moves but he is very stiff.)
Narrator 2: He was so old; he was no longer able to hunt for fish.
Narrator 3: The crane was so hungry, he couldn't bear any linger and he became to cry.
Crane: *(sobs)* Boo, hoo.
Narrator 1: A crab passed by slowly and saw the crying crane.
Crab: Crane, whatever is the matter?
Crane: I'm hungry.
Crab: Why don't you go hunting for some big juicy fish in the lake?
Crane: I can't because I feel bad because I've eaten so much fish over the years. I have decided that I will fast and go hungry until the day I die.
Crab: I don't understand. Why do you feel guilty today? You have eaten fish all your life.
Crane: Crab, haven't you heard, there will be a drought that will last twelve years. There will be no rain and that means all the fish and other creatures in the lake will die.
Crab: Oh no, there must be some way we can save everyone.
Crane: Well, I've an idea. *(The crane puts his arm around the crab's shoulders and softens his voice.)*. There is a big lake not far from here that it is very large and very deep. It has enough water to last years. I could carry any fish that wants to go one by one to the other lake.
Crab: That's a wonderful idea. I will tell all the fish about your plan. You will be a hero.
Narrator 1: Everyday the crane took a fish to the new lake.
Fish 1: Please, crane takes me to the new lake.
(Fish 2 pushes fish 1 out of the way.)

Fish 2: No, crane take me to the new lake.
Crane: Don't worry everyone will get their turn. Soon all the fish will be gone from this lake.
Narrator 2: However, the crane hadn't taken any of the fish to the new lake instead he took each fish to a quite part of the jungle and eats them for his tea.
Narrator 2: One day, the crab asked the crane to take him to the new lake.
Crane: I'm tired of eating fish. Maybe I will try crab today. *(He whispers to the audience.)* Of course, I will take you. Hop into my mouth.
Crab: Crane, we have been flying for a long time. Where is this new lake? I thought it was nearby.
Crane: You foolish crab. There is no lake you shouldn't have trusted me. I'm going to eat you like I've eaten all the other fish.
Crab: Oh no, you are not. *(The crab jumps up and grabs the crane by the neck. The crane passes out.)* I better go back to the lake and warn the other fish about the crafty crane.
Narrator 3: The crab made his way back to the lake as fast as he could.
Fish 3: Crab, why did you come back? Did you not like the new lake?
Fish 4: Where is the crane? Why did he not come back?
Fish 5: We will die if the crane doesn't help us. What will do now?
Crab: One question at a time.
All Fish: What happened?
Crab: The crane didn't want to save us. He wasn't taking the fish to another lake but to a lonely place in the jungle and eating them for his tea. I found out about his evil ways and saved myself. Don't worry he will never bother us again.
Fish: Thank you, crab. You saved our lives.
Narrator 2: The crab was right; the crane never bothered the fish again.
Narrator 3: The crab and the fish lived happily ever after in their lake.

Julie Meighan

The Donkey and the Jackal

Characters: Three Storytellers, Donkey, Jackal, Washerman, Farmer, Farmer's Wife.

Storyteller 1: Once upon a time there lived a donkey.
Storyteller 2: He was a washerman's donkey.
Storyteller 3: Everyday, the donkey carried the washer man's bags of clothes.
Washerman: Come on donkey, you are very strong. You can carry another bundle of clothes to the river.
(The washer man puts bags of clothes on to the donkeys back.)
Donkey: I work so hard during the day.
Washerman: If you work hard during the day, donkey you can relax at night.
Storyteller 1: Every night, the donkey would relax by grazing in a nearby field.
Storyteller 2: One night the donkey met a jackal while he was relaxing in the field.
Jackal: Hello donkey, what are you doing?
Donkey: I am relaxing in this field because I work so hard during the day.
Jackal: May I join you?
Donkey: Of course.
Storyteller 3: The two animals became very good friends and met each other every night.
Donkey: Hello my friend, good to see you.
Jackal: Good to see you do Donkey.
Donkey: What shall we do tonight?
Jackal: Let's go to the nearby farm. If we break the fence, you can graze on the farmer's juicy vegetables which I can feed on some nice juicy chickens.
(They go to the farm and the jackal chases the chickens and the donkey eats the vegetable.)
Storyteller 1: Every night, the jackal and the donkey ate until their stomachs' were full.

Storyteller 2: One night when the two were in the farmer's field, the donkey said…

Donkey: What a lovely quiet night. I feel like singing.

Jackal: Donkey that would be a big mistake… We are thieves so we must be silent. Besides your voice is not sweet or pleasant. You will wake the farmer and he will chase us away.

Storyteller 3: The Donkey was not pleased by what the jackal had said.

Donkey: Jackal, you don't appreciate sweet music because you have lived in the wild too long. Let me show you.

Storyteller 1: The donkey opened his mouth to sing and the jackal shouted…

Jackal: NOOOOOOOOOOOOO! Please don't sing. Let's just eat and leave quietly. No one will know that we were here.

Storyteller 2: The donkey was very insulted by what the jackal had said and he started to get angry.

Donkey: You know nothing about music, Jackal.

Jackal: Well donkey, you can sing but please let me leave before you start.

Storyteller 3: The jackal left the field and the donkey began to sing.

Donkey: Hee haw, hee haw, hee haw.

Storyteller 2: The farmer and the farmer's wife were sleeping soundly in the bed when they were woken by the donkey's singing.

Farmer: What is that dreadful noise?

Farmer's wife: I don't know but you must make it stop.

(The farmer looks out the window and sees the donkey.)

Farmer: Look, there is a donkey in our vegetable field.

Farmer's wife: Make this noise stop now.

(The farmer creeps up behind the donkey. He hits him over the head with a stick.)

Donkey: *(looks around in shock)* what did you do that for?

Farmer: To stop you singing.

Farmer's wife: I have never heard such a noise. We can't sleep.

Storyteller 3: The farmer finds a stone and ties it around the donkey's neck.

Farmer: That will stop you, now, leave my farm.

Storyteller 1: The donkey drags himself out of the field eventually.

Storyteller 2: The jackal was waiting for him outside.

Jackal: Why did you not listen to me?
Donkey: I'm sorry; I should have listened to you. There will be no more juicy vegetables and chicken for us ever again.
Storytellers: The moral of the story is there is always a proper time and place for doing things.

The Jackal and the Elephant

Characters: Three storytellers, jackal, tiger, dead elephant, lion, cheetah.

Storyteller 1: There once a small jackal that lived in the jungle.
Storyteller 2: He moved around the jungle looking for food.
Storyteller 3: He came across an elephant. The elephant was dead. *(Jackal examines and prods the elephant to make sure he is dead.)*
Jackal: I'm so lucky I found this dead elephant. I don't have to hunt for months.
Storyteller 1: He tired to bite into the elephant.
Jackal: The elephant's skin is too tough. I can't cut the skin with my teeth.
Storyteller 2: A lion past by.
Lion: Hello Jackal, what are you doing here?
Jackal: I found a dead elephant and I would like to offer him to you as a sign of my respect your majesty. *(The jackal bows. The lion looks pleased.)*
Lion: I only eat what I hunt.
Jackal: But you are king of the jungle.
Lion: Thank you for offering to me I will leave it for you to enjoy.
Jackal: What will I do now? How will I get to the flesh?
Storyteller 3: A tiger past by.
Tiger: Hello Jackal, what do we have here?
Jackal: A dead elephant but before you sink you teeth into him you must know I'm only guarding it for the lion.
Tiger: Where is the lion?
Jackal: In the river.
Tiger: I'm off before the lion comes back and kills me. Thank you, Jackal.
Storyteller 1: Soon a cheetah past by.
Cheetah: Hello Jackal, what do we have here?
Jackal: The elephant was killed by the lion. He has asked me to guard it.
Cheetah: Where is the lion?

Jackal: In the river.

Cheetah: I'm off before the lion comes back and kills me. Thank you, Jackal.

Storyteller 3: The jackal knew he needed some help to bite through the elephant.

Jackal: Wait, if you want, you can have a quick bite before the lion comes back.

Cheetah: Are you mad? The lion will be really angry if I took a bite.

Jackal: Oh, Cheetah you are my friend. Let me stand guard while you have a bit of the dead elephant. I will shout when I see the lion coming back.

Cheetah: I will take a bite but you need to warn me when the lion is coming.

Jackal: *(Looks at the audience)* He has done what I wanted but now it is time to scare him off. *(Shouts.)* Run, run the lion is coming.

Storyteller 1: The cheetah ran off.

Jackal: Now, I can have the elephant all to myself.

(He starts to eat the elephant.)

Storyteller 2: The moral of the story is …

Storyteller 3: Mental strength is more powerful than physical strength.

The Thief, the Brahmin and the Demon

Characters: Three storytellers, thief, Brahmin, demon, merchant, cow.

Storyteller 1: Once upon a time there lived a very poor Brahmin
Storyteller 2: One day he performed a Pooja in a rich merchant's house.
Merchant: Brahmin, please take this cow as a sign of my appreciation. You could sell his milk at the market and make some money.
Brahmin: Thank you very much, merchant. I will take care of the cow,
Storyteller 3: The Brahmin fed the cow lots of food. He milked the cow everyday and sold the milk at the market.
Storyteller 1: One day a thief was passing by the Brahmin's house. He saw the Brahmin milking the cow.
Thief: What a plump cow, He has lots of milk. I shall steal the cow tonight and have the cow and his milk all to myself.
Storyteller 2: As night fell, the thief quietly crept towards the Brahmin's house.
Storyteller 3: Suddenly, there was a crashing noise and a lighting flash. A demon appeared.
Thief: Who are you and what do you want?
Demon: I'm a demon and I'm very hungry. I want to eat you.
Storyteller 1: The thief thought quickly.
Thief: STOP! Don't eat me. I'm going to the Brahmin's house to steal his cow. You could eat him. He is much fatter than me.
Demon: That's a good idea. You are a little skinny.
(They creep slowly and quietly over the Brahmin wall and into his house. The Brahmin is fast asleep and the cow is asleep next to him.)
Demon: Thief, you were right. What a fat, juicy Brahmin. He looks so delicious. I'm going to eat him straight away.
(He goes to grab the Brahmin, but the thief drags him back.)

Thief: No, you need to wait. I will take the cow first and then you can eat the Brahmin.
Demon: I'm hungry now. I will eat the Brahmin first and then you can take the cow. The cow's mooing will wake the Brahmin and I will lose my dinner.
Storyteller 2: The argument started to get louder and louder.
Thief: No, I'll take the cow first.
Brahmin: No, I'll eat the Brahmin first.
Thief: No, I'll take the cow first.
Brahmin: No, I'll eat the Brahmin first.
Thief: No, I'll take the cow first.
Brahmin: No, I'll eat the Brahmin first.
Storyteller 3: The Brahmin woke up?
Brahmin: What are you doing here? Your quarrelling woke me up.
Thief: This is the demon he wants to eat you.
Demon: This is the thief he wants to steal your cow.
Storyteller 1: The Brahmin used the power of prayer to banish the demon.
Brahmin: Please god, get rid of this demon.
Storyteller 2: The demon vanished.
Thief: What happened to the demon?
Brahmin: God has got rid of the demon and now I will get rid of you.
(He picks up a stick and chases the thief out of his house.)
Storyteller 3: The Brahmin was so happy that he saved his life and the life of his cow.
Storytellers: The moral of the story is - don't quarrel as it always benefits others.

The Owl and Crow

Characters: Three storytellers, the owl, the crow, the owl's wife, the cuckoo, the crane, the swan, the dove, the peacock, the parrot and as many Brahmins and other birds as you want.

Storyteller 1: Once upon a time all the birds in the forest decided to have a meeting.
Storyteller 2: All the birds turned up. *(Birds enter stage one by one.)* There was the cuckoo, the crane, the swan, the dove, the parrot, the peacock and the owl.
Storyteller 3: The only bird missing was the crow.
Cuckoo: Are we all here?
Crane: *(counts)* Yes, all the birds are present.
Swan: *(counts again)* Wait a minute! The crow is missing.
Dove: We must wait for him.
Peacock: We can't wait any longer. We have a very important matter to discuss today.
Cuckoo: We must choose a king of all birds.
Parrot: The bird that is chosen must be able to protect us.
Dove: I know who we should choose.
All birds: Who?
Dove: The owl.
Peacock: That's a very good idea. He is very powerful.
Cuckoo: And he can see at night so he can protect us from other animals.
Crane: And hunters when we are sleeping.
Swan: Hands up if you think the owl should King of all Birds. *(All the birds put up their hands and the parrot counts the hands.)*
Parrot: That is settled. Owl, would you be the king of the birds?
Owl: I would be honoured.
Dove: That settles it then. You will be crowned later today.
Owl: I must go home and tell Mrs. Owl she will be so pleased.
Storyteller 1: The birds prepared a lavish throne.

Storyteller 2: They invited all the Brahmins to come, chant and beat their drums.
(Enter Brahmins chanting and beating drums.)
Storyteller 3: Everything was prepared, when suddenly the crow swooped down and shouted.
Crow: Stop!
(Everyone freezes.)
Crow: What is going on here? What is the reason for this lavish celebration?
Swan: We have decided we need a king of the birds.
Peacock: We all agreed that the Owl is the bird for the job and we are preparing for his coronation.
Crow: Do you really think this is a good idea. The owl is blind by day so he will be no use to anyone. Besides the owl is so very ugly. There are much more beautiful birds than him. Look at the stunning peacock, the colourful parrot and the graceful swan. Who wants an ugly king?
(Birds shake their heads.)
Dove: He has a point.
Cuckoo: Do we really need a king?
Parrot: What will gain from having the owl as our king?
Crow: Absolutely nothing.
Birds: You are right, let's go home.
Storyteller 1: The birds and the Brahmins left, the crow stayed perched on a branch.
Storyteller 2: The owl and his wife arrived for the coronation.
Storyteller 3: But everyone had left.
Owl: What happened?
Owl's wife: Where did everyone go?
Crow: I told them they had no reason to elect you as their king. You are ugly and blind.
Owl: Crow, you are so wicked. I will never be friends with you again. From now on the owls will be sworn enemies of the crows.
Owl's wife: Let's go home.
Crow: Why did I have to speak my mind? The birds were happy to crown the owl as their king. I should have kept my mouth closed. Now, the crows will always have the might owl as their enemies.

The Bug and the Flea

Characters: Three storytellers, bug, flea, king, servant.

Storyteller 1: In India, a long time ago, there lived a king.
Storyteller 2: His palace was very beautiful
Storyteller 3: But by far, his favourite room was his lavish bedroom.
(Enters King, looking very proudly around his bedroom.)
King: *(Yawns)* I think it is time for bed. *(He gets into bed and starts snoring.)*
Storyteller 3: However, what the king didn't know was that inside the folds of the exquisite white satin sheets lived a flea,
Storyteller 1: Every night the flea would suck the king's blood while he was asleep.
(Flea makes sucking sounds.)
Flea: I'm so lucky to live in this exquisite sheet and I can suck the king's blood whenever I'm thirsty.
King: *(wakes up and stretches)* I had a wonderful sleep. *(He gets out bed.)* Now, it is time to perform my kingly duties. *(Exits the stage.)*
Storyteller 2: One day a bug crept into the bedroom.
(Enters bug slowly and quietly.)
Bug: What a beautiful bedroom and what exquisite sheets. I think I will stay here for awhile.
Storyteller 3: Suddenly, the flea saw the bug and shouted loudly....
Flea: Shoo, shoo, bug, get out of here at once.
Bug: Flea that is no way to speak to a guest. You should make me feel welcome and offer me some refreshments.
Flea: *(looks at the bug cautiously)* Yes, you are right. Where are my manners? Bug, what would you like to drink?
Bug: The king's blood. I have drunk many different types of blood but never royal blood. I think the king's blood would be sweet and juicy as he eats the best food.
Flea: I only suck on the king's blood when he is asleep. He never knows I'm there. Your bite is sharp and nasty.

Bug: I promise I will let the king go to sleep before I bite him. He will never know.
(Enters king)
King: What a very busy day I had performing my kingly duties. *(Yawns and stretches.)* I can't wait to hop into my beautiful bed and go to sleep.
(King gets into bed)
Storyteller 1: When the bug saw the king, his mouth began to water.
Bug: *(looks at audience)* I can't wait for the king to go sleep. I'm going to bite him now.
(Bug bites the king really hard. King jumps out of the bed screaming.)
King: Ouch! Servant comes here at once.
(Enter servant.)
Servant: *(bows)* Yes, your majesty.
King: Something has bitten me very hard. It is in my bed. Find it and get rid of it, NOW!
Servant: Your wish his my command, your majesty. *(Bows again.)*
(Servant checks the bed closely.)
Storyteller 2: The bug moved quickly to the corner of the bed and hid himself.
Storyteller 3: The flea hid himself in the folds of the sheets. However, it was not long before the servant found him and grabbed him.
Servant: Caught you, you nasty flea. *(He throws the flea out the window.)* Good riddance.
Bug: Bye, bye flea. *(Bug waves at flea.)*
Storytellers: The moral of the story is beware of false promises.

The Turtle and the Two Swans

Characters: Three storytellers, turtle and two swans.

Storyteller 1: Once upon a time, in India, there lived a turtle.
Storyteller 2: Her two best friends were swans.
Storyteller 3: Everyday, the tree friends would play in the lake.
Storyteller 1: One day the turtle said ....
Turtle: The lake is beginning to dry up.
Swan 1: It is turning into a mud pit.
Swan 2: How will we survive here without water?
Turtle: I know there is a lake not far from here. We could move there and have plenty of water.
Swan 1: That's a good idea but Turtle, you can't fly.
Swan 2: And it is too far for you to walk.
Turtle: Find me a strong stick. I can hold on tight to the stick with my mouth. Both of you can hold on to the ends and carry me to the other lake.
Storyteller 2: The swans searched and searched until they found a large strong stick.
Swan 1: Turtle, we will do what you suggest but remember you mustn't open you mouth of you will fall.
Turtle: Of course I won't.
Swan 2: Let's go.
Storyteller 3: The swans flew up into the sky with the turtle holding on very tightly to the stick.
Storyteller 1: The turtle was amazed as she had never seen the countryside from the sky.
Storyteller 2: After they had flown some distance the turtle began to get bored.
Storyteller 3: She decided to chat to her friends and she opened her mouth.
Turtle: Whoaaaaaaaaa!!!!!!!!!!!
Storyteller 1: She fell to the ground. The swans swooped down and picked her up.
Swan 1: Are you hurt?

Turtle: Yes, I'm sorry; I should have listened to you.
Swan 2: Remember you should always listen to the advice of friends,

The Monkey and the Sparrows

Characters: Two storytellers, monkey and two sparrows.

Storyteller 1: Once upon a time there were two sparrows. They lived happily in their own nest on top of a tree.
Storyteller 2: They had worked very hard to build the nest.
Sparrow 1: We are so lucky we have this nest.
Sparrow 2: It will protect us from the winter weather.
Storyteller 1: One day it started to rain very heavily.
(The sparrows huddle together in their nest.)
Storyteller 2: Soon, a monkey past by.
Monkey: I'm so cold and wet.
Sparrow 1: Monkey, why don't you build a nice warm nest like ours to protect yourself from all weather.
Storyteller 1: The monkey was not happy with a sparrow.
Monkey: Oh Sparrows, why can't you be quiet and mind your own business.
Sparrow 2: It was only a suggestion. We do not suffer from either heat or cold.
Storyteller 2: The monkey started to get angrier.
Sparrow 1: If you made a nest like ours you would be protected.
Sparrow 2: It is very easy to make.
Monkey: *(looks at audience)* I wish they would stop. I'm tired, cold and hungry. I do not need their advice.
Storyteller 1: However, the sparrows ignored the monkey and continued chirping.
Sparrows: Chirp, chirp, chirp…
Storyteller 2: The monkey climbed to the top of the tree and tore the nest to pieces.
(Sparrows look shocked.)
Sparrows: Why did you do that?
Monkey: You are so annoying.
Sparrows: We were only trying to help.

Monkey: I didn't ask for your advice or your help. Now you don't have anywhere to live.
Storytellers: The moral of the story is only give advice to those that want or need it.

THE END

www.ingramcontent.com/pod-product-compliance
Lightning Source LLC
LaVergne TN
LVHW041550060526
838200LV00037B/1221